PORTFOLIO KEEPING

A Guide for Students

PORTFOLIO KEEPING

A Guide for Students

Nedra Reynolds

University of Rhode Island

Bedford/St. Martin's   BOSTON ♦ NEW YORK

FOR BEDFORD/ST. MARTIN'S

Developmental Editor: John Sullivan
Production Editor: Arthur Johnson
Production Supervisor: Cheryl Mamaril
Marketing Manager: Karen Melton
Editorial Assistant: Katherine Gilbert
Copyeditor: Barbara Sutton
Cover Design: Donna Lee Dennison
Composition: Annika Tamura
Printing and Binding: Malloy Lithographing, Inc.

President: Charles H. Christensen
Editorial Director: Joan E. Feinberg
Director of Editing, Design, and Production: Marcia Cohen
Managing Editor: Elizabeth M. Schaaf

Library of Congress Catalog Card Number: 99–65248

Manufactured in the United States of America.

k   j

For information, write: Bedford/St. Martin's, 75 Arlington Street, Boston, MA 02116 (617-399-4000)

ISBN: 0–312–19151–0

Preface for Instructors

Portfolio Keeping is a supplement for college composition courses that use a portfolio method. It defines and illustrates various types of portfolios and walks students through the steps of keeping a working folder, choosing the entries, and preparing the final product. Emphasizing reflective learning and assessment, *Portfolio Keeping* helps students with some of the important decisions involved in preparing a portfolio as a culmination of the writing process.

I wanted to write *Portfolio Keeping* after several years of teaching portfolio-based writing courses, convinced that portfolios provide both structure and an important end goal for writing classes and offer students a meaningful purpose for their writing. Because most writing textbooks treat the portfolio in only a few pages (if at all), I saw the need for a thorough but compact volume dedicated to the use of portfolios and the opportunities they provide for both students and teachers of writing.

The brevity of *Portfolio Keeping* makes it affordable and accessible for students as it complements or supports other writing textbooks for the course, especially process rhetorics or a reader and handbook. Other writing textbooks will cover areas of the writing process or rhetorical strategies much more thoroughly than this volume, but *Portfolio Keeping* gives more attention to reflection and assessment, through, for example, the ten "Taking Stock" activities found throughout the text. Most of the "Taking Stock" exercises can be completed in class within about fifteen minutes and ask for both an individual writing task and a collaborative-learning discussion or follow-up. Organized around the rhythm and pace of a typical process writing course, *Portfolio Keeping* should be a quick and easy reference for students, either when working independently outside of class or in workshop settings.

In assigning *Portfolio Keeping* to your students, you have two equally good options. Students will benefit from reading the entire volume early in the course, with reviews of each chapter as appropriate later in the term, or you can assign the first part, "The Process of Portfolio Keeping," during the first two or three weeks of the course and the second part, "From Process to Product: Preparing for Assessment," during the final few weeks. With either approach, the portfolio is the heart of the course. Because many students will be able to read the entire volume in approximately two hours, assignments from *Portfolio Keeping* should fit easily into your course schedule.

A companion volume, *Portfolio Teaching: A Guide for Instructors*, addresses issues for designing and orchestrating a portfolio writing course in some depth, with sections on such topics as teacher portfolios, course planning and routine activities, formative evaluation, and grading the portfolio. Meant to be flexible without being prescriptive, *Portfolio Teaching* will be especially useful for new teachers and instructors new to the portfolio method for teaching and assessing writing. This companion volume models portfolio teaching practices that reflect and integrate the vast literature on writing portfolios and are adaptable to various classroom situations.

Acknowledgments

I was fortunate to have a number of outstanding reviewers on this project: Pat Belanoff, State University of New York at Stony Brook; Patrick Bizzaro, East Carolina University; Marcia Dickson, Ohio State University at Marion; Alfie Guy, New York University; Bill Lamb, Johnson County Community College; Ken Smith, Indiana University, South Bend; Gail Stygall, University of Washington; and Bonnie Sunstein, University of Iowa. Chuck Christensen and Joan Feinberg at Bedford/St. Martin's made this book possible, and John Sullivan offered expert advice. Katherine Gilbert helped gather books and reviews. Arthur Johnson expertly guided the manuscript through production, while Annika Tamura contributed much to the book's design.

Contents

— INTRODUCTION —
Defining Portfolios and Establishing Expectations

Keeping: The act of holding or supporting. Observance of a rule, institution, practice, promise, and so on. Custody, charge, guardianship. In painting, the maintenance of harmony of composition. Agreement, congruity, harmony.
Keep: To take care of, to look after, watch over, tend. To maintain in proper order. To maintain continuously and in proper form and order (a diary, books, and so forth). To celebrate, to observe. Noun: the stronghold of a castle; a jail.
Keeper: One who has charge, care, or oversight of any person or thing. One worth keeping, especially a fish large enough to be legally caught.

Keep at, keep down, keep off, keep to, keep up, for keeps, keep an eye out, keep company, keep watch, keep one's chin up, keep one's eyes open or peeled, keep one's nose clean, keep pace, keep time, keep to oneself, keep in mind . . .

As you read this, you are probably in the first week of a college writing course that relies on the portfolio method for structuring the class and for assessing your work. If you have not been asked to keep a writing portfolio before, my job is to help you feel confident with the portfolio process. If you *are* familiar with portfolios, I hope to introduce you to a wider variety of strategies for making sound decisions and for presenting the best final product you can.

A writing portfolio consists of pieces of writing that represent a writer's best work or most successful projects. Collected over time and across interests, a portfolio showcases a writer's talent and effort and demonstrates his or her ability to make thoughtful choices about content and presentation. It is a final product meant to be shared with others — perhaps to be assessed by a teacher or trained evaluator, to be read by prospective employers, or to be enjoyed by friends or family. Keeping a portfolio will help you to pay attention to *both* the processes and products of writing. It will also help you to keep track of the evolution of each writing project as well as your development as a writer. Portfolios provide a structure for a writing course that will help you attend to your own learning in a thoughtful, reflective way. Through reflective learning, you can focus on your patterns, habits, and preferences as a student and a writer; learn to repeat what works well for you; and develop strategies for addressing or overcoming the parts of writing that frustrate or puzzle you. At the end of a portfolio writing course, then, you will have a record of your writing processes for each major project; a collection of your best works, polished to presentation quality; and a better understanding of both useful writing strategies and ways you learn best.

Not all portfolios emphasize writing, but the writing portfolio has become a popular method of assessment for college classes. Designs vary, but generally a portfolio course requires you to submit a collection of your best writing — those pieces you have revised with the greatest expertise or those in which you have invested a lot of time and energy. In most cases, the portfolio is evaluated, usually for a large percentage of your final grade.

Even if you haven't encountered portfolios in other classes, you may still recognize the term from art or from investing: Artists keep some of their best works in a portable case or folder, ready to display the pieces that represent their interests, potential, or changes over time. Artists show these portfolios to teachers, gallery owners, employers, or to a jury of other artists. Financial managers keep records of stocks, bonds, mutual funds, or other investments to review periodically and to update as needed. In similar versions of portfolio keeping, teachers or faculty members compile portfolios to apply for promotions or to change positions. In every version, the portfolio is not static but changes according to recent achievements, expanded ideas, or new interests.

Because writing students often experience new interests or expanded ideas during the course, portfolios offer a flexible structure for recording those changes or pursuits. Writing students who keep portfolios learn to practice reflection, a form of critical thinking, and learn to analyze and respond appropriately to a variety of rhetorical situations. Your portfolio writing course will emphasize the writing process, especially revision, because portfolios provide a context and good reason to revise. The demand of collecting and presenting your best work will help you begin to understand the number of drafts sometimes required for a piece of writing to become focused, organized, and clear. Because writing is a very complex act, one of the most challenging and sophisticated activities humans engage in, writers need time to improve and to build confidence. Portfolios create a bigger window of time for writers to practice before the writing must be evaluated.

The portfolio method often postpones grades on papers until the end of the course, giving you time to develop and room to take risks, but portfolios do not neglect the importance of a polished final product. Even though a portfolio writing class concentrates on invention, drafting, reader response, revision, and editing — and gives time for your skills to develop before the writing "counts" — the writing does, ultimately, count.

Portfolio Keeping will help as you sort through assignments and projects and make the kinds of complex or subtle decisions that all writers make. Throughout this guide you will find advice and strategies to help you keep track of your learning and make solid, reasoned choices about your portfolio's contents and appearance. Your tasks as a portfolio keeper will include tending to your developing ideas, keeping watch over your own learning patterns, helping your peers or collaborators, and being responsible for the final product. In a portfolio writing course, you'll need to save all of your drafts and notes in a working folder, keep track of your choices and changes, and make some important decisions near the end of the term.

In the following section, you'll find definitions of key terms or phrases that you might encounter in your portfolio course as well as descriptions of the many types of portfolios and their various forms or uses. Understanding some of the principles of writing portfolios will give you a good start on your writing course and will make you aware of the importance of reflective learning.

DIFFERENT TYPES OF PORTFOLIOS

Although they share many features or principles, portfolios do vary. Portfolios for educational purposes are usually of two broad types — learning portfolios and assessment portfolios — and they share the principles of choice, reflection, and variety.

Portfolios for Learning

Some approaches to portfolios are specifically for the benefit of students, with or without some evaluation of their work. If you are asked to keep a learning portfolio, you are invited to keep, collect, and create a portfolio for your own benefit, not to prove to teachers, coaches, or supervisors that you should pass a course, receive an award, or get a promotion. Learning portfolios invite students to collect or create a variety of artifacts — essays, photographs, charts, letters, and so on — that best represent their experiences and engagement with the learning process in a particular subject area. Two examples of learning portfolios are described in the following sections, but if you are asked to keep a learning portfolio in your writing course, remember that the degree of freedom you are given will require savvy choices. In addition, after keeping a learning portfolio for several weeks, you may be asked to turn your learning portfolio into an evaluation portfolio.

Portfolios for Evaluation, Assessment, or Testing

An evaluation portfolio, like a learning portfolio, also promotes and sustains learning, but it shifts the attention, at a certain point, from the learning process to a final product. These types of portfolios vary widely, but they share a similar goal: to show someone else what the portfolio keeper has learned, or to convince an audience of the portfolio keeper's achievements, abilities, or talents. An artist puts together a portfolio to show to gallery owners or employers, or a writing major designs a portfolio to show to editors or graduate program directors. Similarly, students in a variety of courses keep portfolios to show the instructor, at semester's end, what they have learned from the course and applied to their portfolio's contents.

Whether a learning or assessment portfolio, these three major principles define writing portfolios for most situations: choice, reflection, and variety.

- **Choice** Well-designed portfolios give the writer room to choose what to include and how to arrange and present the entries. If portfolio keepers are "told" what to include, where to do so, and in what form, there won't be nearly as much "learning" in the process. Keepers of *learning* portfolios make dozens of choices. Keepers of *assessment* portfolios also make many choices, often different ones. While writers make choices, selections, or decisions at every stage of the writing process — some of them unconscious or hardly recognized — the portfolio method allows some of those choices to be more conscious. No matter what type of portfolio you'll be keeping for this writing course, you will need to choose wisely. Helping you to inform those choices is one of the purposes of this guide.

- **Reflection** Portfolios let you look at your writing in a different way, taking into account a full semester's work rather than just one assignment. Also sometimes called *reflective learning* or *self-assessment*, this part of the portfolio method asks you to take a careful look at your patterns, strengths, and preferences for negotiating writing tasks, for learning a new skill, or for practicing a complex set of skills like those required for reading and writing. Almost every form of the portfolio method of assessment asks that you go a step beyond putting the portfolio together: You need to be able to articulate *why* you made certain choices or what those choices are meant to convey. Educational theorists might use the word *meta-cognition* to describe the ability of students to think about their own thinking. *Meta* means "after," "behind," or "beyond"; *cognition* means "the act or process of knowing." Thus *meta-cognition* is the ability to "know beyond one's knowing," or to think about your own thinking, usually after an assignment or task has been completed.

- **Variety** Because portfolio keepers will have different strengths and different interests, portfolios try to celebrate and cultivate these differences. A writing portfolio invites you to show off your writing abilities across different kinds of assignments, for different audiences, or with different amounts of time spent on each entry. Variety is one of the reasons that portfolios are considered a more "valid" measurement of a person's writing ability, especially as compared with a timed, multiple-choice test on grammar, usage, punctuation, and mechanics. When teachers see a portfolio, they see more than one sample, and they see pieces written at different times.

Within these principles of choice, reflection, and variety, writing portfolios can have several differences. Your instructor will let you know which type of portfolio you will be keeping for this course. Some common variations on the portfolio method for writing classes follow, but note that, because portfolios are a very flexible teaching tool, not all of the possibilities are covered.

- **A writing folder** You are asked to submit all drafts, notes, outlines, scribbles, doodles, and messy pages, representing all your writing, finished or unfinished. Everything is saved, if only for simple record keeping, but you may also be asked to select from the folder two or three of your most promising pieces to revise for a "presentation" portfolio (see page 6). In a first-year composition class, for example, Frederick is expected to bring his writing folder to each class meeting. He buys a notebook that has several pockets bound together and labels each pocket with the project number and a brief description of the assignment. His instructor often asks students to refer to specific documents in the folder in order to write a journal entry or to complete a class activity. In another case, a technical writing instructor asks that students submit, along with each final product, a complete record of the writing process that led to that product. This means that Tina needs to keep hard copies of all of her notes, drafts, outlines, peer reviews, and photocopied articles in order to show the instructor evidence of her discovery, drafting, and research process. The key feature of writing folders is that they include "everything" related to a project or course, and the contents demonstrate how much collecting, drafting, and revising the writer has done.

- **A learning or open portfolio** Not necessarily submitted for assessment purposes, this type of portfolio gives you the opportunity to submit a variety of materials that have contributed to your learning of the course material or subject matter. You have the freedom to determine the portfolio's contents and how the contents will be presented or organized. Keepers of learning portfolios may choose a variety of documents to demonstrate what and how they learned, including photos or both print and nonprint artifacts. For example, in a course on writing with computers, Tyler prepares a learning portfolio with these electronic entries that he submits to his instructor on a disk: (1) a transcript from one of his online discussions with members of the class; (2) another transcript from a public listserv he joined early in the semester; (3) three of the many e-mails he exchanged with the instructor; and (4) his Web site address. When the instructor visits his Web site, she sees evidence of his notes, drafts, and final version for each of the major projects. Open portfolios work well for a variety of courses. For example, Sheila keeps a learning portfolio for her beginning ballet class. She includes a videotape of her work at the barre during the second week, seventh week, and fifteenth week, and she writes an accompanying explanation of the improvements her instructor should notice. She also submits a journal, written for herself in twice-weekly entries, about her sore legs, blistered toes, and improved posture as well as her elation at being praised in class for the first time. Sheila's learning portfolio also includes a research paper on the dancer Natalia Makarova and a ticket stub from a performance by the American Ballet Theatre. Sheila's learning portfolio for her ballet class is not limited to written materials, to projects assigned by the instructor, or to activities done in class. She chooses a variety of items that demonstrate *how* she learned (not just *what* she learned) in beginning ballet.

- **A closed portfolio**   Often used for assessment purposes, this type of portfolio gives you guidance in what to submit. You have fewer options but still need to make decisions, to show as much variety as possible within the guidelines, and to demonstrate your ability to look critically on your work. For example, for an introductory American literature course, the instructor asks students to submit these items: (1) a revision of the comparison/contrast essay on two short stories; (2) an explication of an unassigned contemporary poem in the anthology; and (3) one of the two essay exams written in class (the actual blue book), along with an explanation of how students would rewrite the exam or change their responses. As a preface to their three portfolio entries, Taylor and her classmates are asked to explain their choices and to make a case for what they have learned about American literature. From the portfolios, turned in during the last week of classes, the instructor will create the final exam questions.

- **A midterm portfolio**   You are able to give the portfolio method a trial run, or the midterm grade is determined by one or two papers being sub-mitted for evaluation, perhaps accompanied by a brief self-assessment. For example, in a research writing course designed around collaborative projects, the instructor requests a midterm portfolio instead of a midterm exam. Each group is asked to write via e-mail a collaborative proposal to the instructor about which assignment they will be entering and why. After receiving their instructor's approval to submit their informative paper about changes in libraries in the last five years, Group 1 revises and edits in response to comments received from the instructor and the other groups. Group 1 then writes a brief statement to the class about what their submission demonstrates about their increasing understanding of research. Finally, Group 1 submits the midterm portfolio electronically to the course Web page, where all of the students in the course will be able to read Group 1's submission and make comments.

- **A final or presentation portfolio**   At the end of the course you submit the portfolio — revised, edited, and polished to presentation quality — and it is evaluated to determine a significant portion of your final grade for the course. (This type of portfolio may overlap with the closed port-folio or other types, but the difference is the emphasis on *polish*.) For instance, with three weeks remaining in the term, Miguel sits down one evening and spreads the contents of his working folder across a large table. For the final portfolio in his expository writing class, he needs to choose two of the longer, formal projects to revise and three of the shorter, informal assignments. After quickly rereading all of his pieces, Miguel settles on his literacy narrative and an argumentative essay, along with a journal entry, a letter to another writer in the class, and a reading response. Because every entry in this portfolio needs to be finished to the best of his ability, Miguel next has to decide what specific changes will improve each piece the most. After planning some of these, Miguel makes a time-management chart so that he can stay on schedule and allow himself sufficient time to edit, proofread, and polish each entry in his presentation portfolio.

- **A modified or combination portfolio** Many portfolio designs fall under this category. You are offered some choices but also have some requirements to fulfill. For the writing classes I teach, for example, portfolio keeping leads to a final, presentation-quality collection that is neither purely "closed" nor "open," but somewhere in between. In my first-year composition courses, a typical portfolio requirement is that students keep a writing folder throughout the term; then they choose which three writing projects (out of five or six) they wish to revise and edit for portfolio presentation. Along with the three projects, students choose from the writing folder any three to five pages that best represent their learning or their writing strengths, improvement, or interests. These three to five pages may be brief in-class writings, journal entries, writer's memos (or what I call "postwrites"), or reading-response pieces, and the selections will vary for each student, giving the portfolio variety and individuality. This portfolio assignment is "open" in that students choose what pieces to include, but it is also "closed" in that I ask for a specific number of entries or limit the number of pages.

Now that you have a better understanding of how portfolios can differ and how they are often used in composition or other writing-intensive courses, the next section will introduce you to portfolio keeping. Before moving on, however, take the time to complete the following task.

TAKING STOCK #1: Establishing Expectations

After receiving the course syllabus from your instructor and picking up your books at the bookstore, review your syllabus and textbooks carefully, especially the course policies, procedures, assignments, and expectations. Then write one or two paragraphs about your previous experiences with portfolios or how you expect to do in this course. What assignments or activities do you think you will do well on and why? What assignments or activities do you think will be difficult for you and why? What parts of your reading and writing history make you confident about some parts of the course and hesitant about others?

Check with your instructor about whether to turn in this piece. Otherwise keep it in your working folder; it may come in handy later.

PART ONE

THE PROCESS OF PORTFOLIO KEEPING

—1—
Setting Goals and Planning Ahead

By the end of the **first week** of class, you should understand your instructor's plan for the portfolio method. Is the portfolio being collected at the end of the course, at midterm, or at both times? Is the portfolio best described as a writing folder, a closed portfolio, or some combination? To make sure that your understanding matches your instructor's intentions, see if you can answer each of the following questions. (Regardless of whether you write your answers in a journal or a notebook or post them on the course Web page, be sure to **keep a copy** for reference later.)

1. How many papers can be included?
2. Do **I** make all of the choices about what to include? Will anyone help me make these choices? Will the instructor tell me what to include?
3. Do all the papers I include need to be revised? If so, what level, quality, or extent of revision is expected?
4. How much of the course grade is determined by the portfolio grade?
5. Are the portfolio entries graded separately, or does the entire portfolio receive one grade?
6. May I include papers written for other courses?
7. May I include entries other than texts or documents; that is, may I include photographs, videos, maps, diskettes with downloaded Web pages, or other visual aids?
8. Is the portfolio prefaced by a cover letter or introductory essay? Does each entry need a separate cover sheet? Is reflection or self-assessment expected, or are description and explanation adequate?

In addition to having all of the necessary information about how to succeed in your portfolio course, you can also think ahead about how you want to achieve choice, variety, and reflection in your portfolio, or how you might want to present yourself as a writer.

- Do you want to show *progress,* how much your writing and thinking has improved?
- Do you want to show *persistence,* your ability to stick with a project for a long period?
- Do you want to show *flexibility,* that you can write in different styles or voices?
- Do you want to show *creativity,* how you have made the assignments your own?
- Do you want to show *independence,* that you have revised well beyond the suggestions or made considerably more changes than were recommended?

You needn't be able to answer these questions now, but having goals for the course is a good idea, even though you may change or adapt them later. Your instructor may ask that you set some goals once the class is in a routine or as soon as writing projects have been taken through each stage of the writing process. Some writing teachers use "contracts" to help students set and meet certain goals; these contracts are tailored to students' writing strengths, but they also address weaknesses head-on. Even if your instructor does not ask you to fill out a contract or to set specific goals, in the list that follows, check off the goals that best represent what you would like to accomplish in this course.

___ I hope to keep up with all assignments and stay on top of things, not fall behind.

___ I want to become more comfortable with sharing my writing with others.

___ I want to learn more about writing with computers.

___ I'd like to organize my thoughts better.

___ Sometimes when I write, I know what I want to say, but it doesn't come out the way I want it to. I'd like to know how to fix that.

___ I'd like to be able to take constructive criticism without feeling defensive.

___ I want to find out if my writing skills are strong enough to do well in college or to choose a career that involves writing.

___ I want to write forceful arguments that convince people without offending them.

___ I'd like to be able to read over a draft and know what to do to make it better.

___ I want to try to write every day in a journal.

___ I want to figure out why some of my essays go so smoothly and some are so difficult.

___ I want to be proud of my portfolio and sure that I did my best possible work.

Other goals:

_____

_____

—2—

Keeping Track and Staying Organized

Once you are clear about the expectations and procedures of your portfolio course, and you have established some goals or begun the process of reflective learning, you are ready to begin keeping your working folder, the first step toward a successful portfolio. You may or may not have received the assignment for the first writing project, but don't wait long to begin planning strategies for staying organized. You'll have a better experience with portfolio keeping if you take some time in the **first or second week** to start your working folder.

If you are generally an organized person, you might have an edge on portfolio keeping. If you aren't as organized as you would like to be, there's hope. Start thinking about how organized you usually are, or write a short piece about your usual habits for trying to stay organized. Do you keep a calendar or date book, carry it with you, consult it, and record appointments or due dates religiously? Do you keep separate notebooks or folders for each class? When you get ready to study for a test or to write an assignment, are you generally able to locate everything you need, or do you spend a lot of time looking and gathering materials? Depending on how organized you are, you may have to give more or less attention to the working folder.

Keeping *all* of your materials from a writing class may be new to you if you have not used a portfolio method before. In a portfolio writing class, returned papers are not forgotten papers. In other classes or in high school, your written assignments may have been returned with comments, grades, or both, but they were considered "finished" by you and the teacher. Because the teacher did not expect to see the paper again, you weren't sure what to do with it. You stuck these papers in the back of a spiral notebook, or on a shelf of your bookcase, or in your locker or car, and then you threw them out when the course was over or when you were on a cleaning binge. The practice of *not* saving papers is understandable if they don't need to be saved (and if you're not sentimental about them), but keeping a portfolio means becoming a saver.

For the portfolio method, you need to *hang on to your stuff* so that you can sort through all the returned papers and decide which to revise and submit in the portfolio. Your assignments may still come back with grades or comments (or both), but that doesn't mean the process is over. With the portfolio method, you need to keep returned assignments and to keep track of your writing (and learning) for the length of the course. Although being organized or keeping paperwork or electronic files in order might not come naturally to you, it will help tremendously if you can cultivate that habit for your portfolio writing course.

No matter how you approach being organized, the bottom line is to keep everything. Keeping is the name of the game, so don't throw anything away or delete anything related to the course. Keep all of your notes, lists, drafts, outlines, clusters, responses from readers, photocopied articles, and references for works cited pages.

So that all of this "keeping" doesn't get out of control, you need to begin to design a storage system that helps you to identify and locate what's what. You need to devise a system for locating things quickly and recognizing what they are. A working folder can help.

KEEPING A WORKING FOLDER

A working folder houses all the work that you do prior to selecting pieces for the portfolio. It might be a file folder or notebook that holds all of your materials — paper or electronic — related to the writing projects of this course: A working folder contains all the notes, assignments or handouts from class, outlines, drafts, peer responses, and teacher feedback. If your writing class works mostly on computers, see the next section of this chapter, "Keeping on a Computer." If using printed copies allows you to stay more organized, however, invest in a good organizer or notebook, one that will withstand the wear and tear of backpacks or book bags and your busy life. Reserve this binder or folder for this course only because you'll be surprised at how quickly the stuff will accumulate.

One option is to buy a cardboard accordion-type file folder, usually found with pockets labeled in alphabetical order. This kind of storage system will stand up on your desk or on the floor and makes it easy to find a certain draft or returned paper. Another option is a binder with several pocket folders. Whatever your choice, date and label everything that you put in it, and make sure that each pocket or file folder has a name.

Your labels might resemble some of these:

- Discovery drafts of first paper
- Notes from field observation

- Summary of *New York Times* article, returned with comments
- Peer response forms — Paper 3
- Draft of complaint letter
- Ideas for Web page design

Other logical ways of organizing your working folder would be to label or sort according to (1) chronology, (2) topic, or (3) your own level of interest in each project. For example, your labels might read:

Assignment 1, drafts and notes

Assignment 1, professor's comments

Assignment 2, drafts and outline

Assignment 2, peer response forms

Assignment 2, professor's comments (and so on)

or

Review of the Literature for Research Project

Analysis of three Imus shows

Informed argument about radio talk shows

or

Favorite paper so far (Assignment 3)

Papers I could revise

Papers I hate

How you label the contents of your working folder is up to you, but some kind of labeling and regular efforts to keep the contents organized will help you tremendously later on.

TAKING STOCK #2: Getting Organized

After you have started your working folder, meet with a small group of your classmates to compare working folders and ideas for staying organized. How have your group members designed their storage systems or methods of keeping track of drafts and assignments? Which of their "get organized" techniques are new to you or different from yours? Borrow the best ideas you collect, and incorporate them into your working folder.

KEEPING ON A COMPUTER

Portfolio keeping takes place on or with computers in a couple of different ways. Like most writers today, students use a word processing program (for example, Microsoft Word) and save their writing to a hard drive and a diskette, expediting the revision and editing process. Students also may be enrolled in writing classes in which electronic writing technologies are a major feature of the course; these students may post their essays to a course Web site or other Internet location and may not be using or producing much paper. At my university, for example, six or eight sections of writing are taught as virtual courses or as Web-based writing courses, where the course meets online instead of or in addition to meeting in a classroom. For approximately 160 students each semester, therefore, portfolio keeping is going to be largely electronic in nature (though for many other students portfolio keeping will be minimally electronic). With the advantages of electronic writing technologies come problems, so electronic portfolio keeping also requires careful storage, saving, and labeling.

Every writer will at one time or another suffer the agony of losing files, but your losses can be minimized if you get into the habit now of **saving or backing up everything you write**, religiously, regularly, and frequently. (Make sure to enable the AutoSave feature of your word processing program.) After composing a great sentence, use the mouse to click on "Save." After moving a paragraph from the last page to the second page, click on "Save." After painstakingly entering a series of statistics, click on "Save" again. Then, at the end of a drafting or revising session on the computer, save to a diskette (floppy disk) or to an external tape drive. If you have your own computer, you still need to save your work on diskettes regularly. Investing in an external tape drive (like a Zip drive) is also a good idea because if your hard drive crashes, your files can be restored from the external drive. In addition, when printing difficulties strike — one of the most common problems my students have — at least you know your sentences are safe.

For electronic portfolio keepers, it's vitally important to *save, save, save everything* on floppy disks and by sending files to other locations. If you are portfolio keeping on your own computer, open a folder for your writing course and within it a file for each project assigned — for example, one file for each essay assignment and another file for your journal. Label the files clearly. Besides backing up to diskettes routinely (compulsively), you can also send files to your own or your instructor's e-mail account or to the course Web site. If anything happens to your floppy disks, your files will still be archived elsewhere.

If you use campus or community computers, you won't be able to save your work on the hard drive, so **always have a diskette** and keep an extra blank diskette in your bag or backpack. Similarly, if your class meets in a computer lab, you'll need to have a diskette to save your work, so carrying one or two around all the time is a good idea. If you use a friend's or roommate's computer, you may be able to save on the hard drive, but it's still crucial to make backup copies on diskettes for the inevitable day when the hard drive crashes.

Fundamental to your sanity and success, therefore, is the rule to **save early and save often**. In addition, run your diskettes through a virus check program as often as possible, as campus computers can be virus-prone.

If your writing course is not dependent on electronic writing technologies for the daily work of the class — as most are not — but you are using word processing to draft your projects, your teacher will realize that many of the changes you make on a draft are made onscreen. Nevertheless, you should print hard copies after you make fairly significant changes to a paper. Printing your drafts regularly can help you to see your writing differently, and it will also expedite your record keeping. Many writers, including those who can't imagine writing by hand anymore, appreciate a hard copy or printed version for editing. So, after your paper has changed considerably, print a hard copy for record keeping (to put in the working folder) *and* to edit the text. Even if you are sending your draft electronically to readers, it's a good idea to print a hard copy just in case. As a last resort, if both the hard drive and the floppy disk fail, you will at least have a printout to show the instructor you did the work and also to use to reenter the paper onto the computer, perhaps with more safeguards.

Because the portfolio method for writing courses relies so much on a system of tracing writers' progress or charting writers' improvements, learning how to use the computer wisely will simplify your record keeping, save you time, and help you to present a quality product at the end of the course.

KEEPING TRACK OF COMMENTS OR RESPONSES

Your portfolio process and the final product are influenced immeasurably by your readers: your peer reviewers, your instructor, your friends, roommates, or family members. When someone reads one of your drafts, quickly or carefully, as a favor or as an assigned activity in class, it is important to keep track of reactions, comments, and suggestions. If you wait until the end of the course, when it's time to choose which projects to revise and to submit, you won't remember what your readers said about the piece unless you have recorded their comments.

For example, most student writers will find themselves in the following situation: The instructor returns an essay with comments or suggestions for revision, but class is almost over, and people are packing up and getting ready to leave. The temptation is to stuff the paper in your folder and hurry to your next class or lab, but it's more helpful to take the time to see if you can understand all of the instructor's comments. If you cannot decipher the handwriting on a marginal notation, if it's hard to make an appropriate change, or if you don't understand a suggestion, it will be difficult to know how to improve the paper. If time has run out to ask for clarification, then make an appointment to discuss it further, or send your instructor an e-mail message later in the day.

Before you label the project and file it away, then, make sure you understand your reader's comments. Before the opportunity passes, make some changes in response to the suggestions right away, while the ideas are fresh and the project is still on your mind. Chris, for example, gets her paper back and reads the following comment her teacher has written: "Perhaps you could introduce your grandfather sooner, giving you opportunities to connect this trip to happy childhood memories." Chris isn't sure where to introduce her grandfather before her ninth paragraph, near the end of the piece, and she also doesn't necessarily want her paper to concentrate on childhood memories. Chris stops by during her instructor's office hours that day to present her questions. With the paper in front of them both, the two have a conversation about the grandfather reference and where it fits best, if at all. Between the two of them, they decide that Chris should either introduce the connection to her grandfather much sooner or drop it completely because it is just left hanging in this draft. Chris doesn't decide yet, but before leaving her instructor's office, she makes notes that will help focus her revision if she decides to revise the paper for her portfolio. As Chris did, wait to file the paper away until *after* you are clear about the comments and have one or two ideas for revision. Let it simmer, and when you're ready to work on the piece again, you will have both a plan and some fresh insight. In any case, decide on strategies early for this important record keeping and make sure you can locate the comments of others in your working folder later on.

In addition to saving copies, making backups, and practicing good record keeping, you can also stay organized by managing your time wisely. If time management is always a challenge for you, try scheduling a certain block of time (for example, Wednesday nights from eight to eleven) to work specifically on your portfolio course. Even if you don't have a paper due or a reading assignment, you can take some time to review your returned drafts, make notes toward a reflective piece, or work on organizing your materials.

—3—
Keeping Watch, or Becoming a Reflective Learner

A keeper keeps watch — a lighthouse keeper, a groundskeeper. The reflective portfolio method asks you to keep watch over yourself, to tend to your own learning garden. This section covers ways that you can pay attention to your strengths and weaknesses, your preferences and needs, your best and worst conditions for writing well. Understanding more about yourself as a learner, reader, and writer will help you to make sound choices for your portfolio and to articulate those choices to your readers.

Becoming a reflective learner takes time and practice. Reflective students develop the ability to identify and discuss their choices, strengths, or learning processes; they practice the ability to be insightful, even self-conscious, about their learning. The test of your ability to be reflective will come at the end of the course, usually when the portfolio is due and a reflective essay or introduction is expected. It's better, however, to begin cultivating a reflective writing process very early in the course.

PRACTICING REFLECTIVE LEARNING

For writing and other complex activities, it's important to your improvement to be able to step back and evaluate your performance, to assess what you do well and what you need to work on. Maybe you have great ideas but find it hard to organize them. Maybe you write classic thesis statements but run out of things to say in support of them. Maybe you feel anxious about the part of writing that insists on correctness and perfection — parts like the final editing and the works cited pages. If you can identify these features of your own attitudes and habits, that's the first step toward improvement.

Because portfolio writing classes ask for significant reflection at the end of the course, or when the portfolio is due for evaluation, you will probably be asked to practice reflection throughout the term. You have already begun, in fact, by writing in response to Taking Stock #1 on page 7. Perhaps the most straightforward way of practicing reflection is to try to answer, each week or so, some basic questions about your learning in the course: What am I learning? How am I learning? What is or isn't making sense, coming together, or clicking for me? Sit down once a week or so and think about how the course is going for you. Write informally about that week's course material — what you remember, understand, or could explain to others. Keep track, in just one or two paragraphs, of any small successes (or failures), or record your observations about the pace and quality of the course, about your role within it, and about your goals for the upcoming week.

To make this practice more formalized or systematic, your instructor may assign one or more of the following reflective writing tasks, but if not, get in the habit of reflection early in the course and keep it up throughout the term. Three ways to practice and cultivate reflective learning are:

A Writer's Log or Journal

Writer's Memos or Postwrites

Midterm Self-Assessments or Reflection

A Writer's Log or Journal

Writing or composition classes will often assign or recommend journal keeping because writing informal entries — without worrying about errors or formal features or style — is a good way to learn the material, to rehearse main ideas, to reiterate class discussion, or to respond to class reading material (commonly called a reading-response journal). "Write-to-learn" is the popular phrase for this kind of activity, and many teachers depend on it to reinforce learning — and to ask students to reflect on their learning. Journals or logs can take many forms, such as personal diaries, travel narratives, professional record keeping, and can serve as inexpensive therapy or as rehearsal for writing projects. Generally, journals contain anything that a writer chooses to record, but for the purpose of becoming a more conscientious student of writing, this type of writer's log should be devoted to entries about your writing and learning for this course.

Keeping a writer's log, journal, or daybook is one way to practice a reflective writing process — to keep track of one's writing process, problems, or triumphs, or to jot down possible titles, writing schedules, outlines, and lists. Working writers tend to record how their projects are developing, changing, or frustrating or pleasing them. These informal texts, sometimes handwritten, record a project's evolution and, over a period of time, show patterns and preferences. I tend to use my writer's log to yell at myself about getting a project done or to solve a problem in the text that's bugging me. In reading through my log for evidence of my patterns of working and learning, I find that, for me, the discipline of daily or sustained writing is the most difficult thing or what I struggle with most. To know that about myself means that I must pay close attention, watch for signs that I'm falling behind on a project, and then give myself firm deadlines to get back on track.

Here's an entry from Maria's writer's log:

> I think I'm trying to do way too much in this version. By the time I get to the conclusion, I'm having to summarize too much and cover the same territory again, which may be a sign that I've been over ambitious. Vicky [a peer re-

viewer] hinted that my thesis was too broad, but I didn't want to hear it because I was still very excited about the ideas and still finding plenty to say. Now that I've found more examples and developed most of the major points, I see that I need to go back and sharpen the thesis by dropping my reference to the past views of computers and education. I think the paper will work better without the historical overview, and I'll just concentrate on current uses of computers in education. It seems as though I've done a lot of writing on the history part for nothing, but maybe I can use it for another essay later if I stay interested in it.

Questions to Begin Your Writer's Log

- At what time during the day do you write best or have the most focused concentration?

- Where do you do your best work? Why is that place helpful or inspiring?

- What tools, objects, or things do you like to have around you when you write? When or how did these preferences become apparent to you?

- What do these habits or preferences say about you as a writer? as a learner?

Writer's Memos or Postwrites

Another good method for practicing a reflective writing process is the writer's memo or postwrite. A brief account of the writing process, a reflection on the paper's evolution, and an anticipation of readers' responses, postwrites are written after the essay or piece is well under way, in a draft ready for readers. Though they are often called writer's memos (a memorandum to the reader), I call them "postwrites" because they are written *after* the writing and because "memo" has other forms or purposes. Postwrites support reflective learning: They ask writers to think carefully about their texts before sharing them with others, and they give writers some control over the response process.

Here's how the writer's postwrite works. Before asking others (peer response group members, the instructor, friends) to read your paper and give you feedback, you need to answer some questions (in writing) about your draft: How do you feel about it? What shape do you think it's in? What questions do you have for readers about the paper? In other words, you need to do some work judging your own writing before you ask others to judge. This way, you can move the peer response session along, especially if time is limited, and you can give readers some direction.

Read the sample postwrite on page 20. You'll notice that the questions were designed by the instructor for the writers to answer about their own essays, the processes they went through to produce the current draft, and the feedback or advice they received from readers. Postwrites can take many other forms, however. The instructor doesn't need to write the questions, but the principle remains the same that postwrites are directed to the paper's readers. Postwrites help both writers and readers to get more out of the response process.

WRT 301.02 -- Spring 1999

WRITER'S POSTWRITE for Project 3

To: Dr. Reynolds

From: _____

Re: _____ (title)

1. Summarize your paper in two or three sentences:

2. What key decisions or choices did you make about organizing your narrative, and where do these decisions show up in your text?

3. Of the following narrative techniques, pick one and explain how and where it works especially well in your piece: showing vs. telling; pace; characterization; dialogue; time sequence; a "twist" or surprise.

4. What did your readers say about your title? your introduction or lead? your conclusion? your transitions or flow? Relate some good advice that you received (who gave it), and how you used it to improve your text.

5. How can I help you most in my response to this piece? PLEASE BE SPECIFIC about the parts or passages that you still aren't satisfied with, or a decision you made that you want me to comment on.

SAMPLE POSTWRITE A

How Postwrites Help Writers

Without the discipline or guidance of a postwrite, too many writers will take *any* advice about a paper — or will ignore all of it. Composing a postwrite will help you to identify areas of the draft in which you feel dissatisfied, even if you cannot quite name, let alone "fix," the problem. To alert readers to fuzzy or weak areas will help *them* to help *you*; they may see exactly what the text needs. Composing a postwrite usually includes describing your writing process, identifying the steps you took or a strategy that proved fruitful. These descriptions — one account for each essay you write — will provide a record of how you felt about each essay before readers saw it and will provide excellent practice with reflection — the ability to "see" your own thought processes and decisions. A full set of postwrites may also provide a record of the ways in which your writing process has changed or what steps within your process are most challenging or most rewarding. **Keep** your postwrites in your working folder and review them when you are asked to reflect on your writing and learning processes.

How Postwrites Help Readers

Without being able to read a writer's postwrite, readers will often give generic, unfocused commentary. How many times has someone read your paper and said, "I like it; it's good," but nothing more? When you reply, "Are you sure?" your reader finds a spelling error, but that's about it. Reading a postwrite first will help readers know where to look or will push them to give considered and thorough feedback. Postwrites will concentrate the reader's attention on, for example, your focus, support, or organization so that readers will have more to say to you about what works and what needs work in your draft.

In general, postwrites give writers practice in reflective learning and also ask readers to read in a more focused way. If you don't use postwrites in your class, then for each paper you share in peer response groups, or for each paper your instructor collects, write a log or journal entry about what you think the paper does well and what it still needs. Keep track, in notes you date, label, and save, of the process you went through to plan, research, or draft each paper — where you got stuck and where things clicked. These notes will help jog your memory or will provide you with phrases to use when you are asked to explain your writing process for a particular paper, or when you are asked to write reflectively about your learning.

Another example of a postwrite appears on page 22; it illustrates how the questions may change according to the assignment or the point in the semester. (What doesn't change, in the postwrites I design for my students, is question no. 5.)

WRT 101.42

POSTWRITE QUESTIONS FOR PROJECT 4

Name: _____

Title: _____

1. What problem or issue are you addressing in your proposal, and how did you come up with this topic? If you
   changed topics along the way, when did you switch
   and why?

2. What exactly are you proposing -- a solution or change
   in policy, procedure, or attitude? Who will be interested
   in such a proposal?

3. What is the most important piece of research that
   informs your proposal? Summarize the author's argument in two or three sentences.

4. Name three specific ways that your paper has changed
   since Tuesday's workshop. If you wish, identify someone
   who was very helpful in guiding those changes.

5. How can I help you most in my response to this draft?
   PLEASE BE SPECIFIC about parts or passages that you
   think still need work or that you want me to look at
   carefully. What questions do you have for me as a reader?

SAMPLE POSTWRITE B

Midterm Self-Assessments or Reflection

Even if you don't keep track of your learning and progress regularly, through postwrites or writing logs, it's important to take stock at least at the halfway point — one of the reasons that college instructors are fond of midterm exams. At this point, the class should be in a routine, and certain concepts should be familiar or well established. If you've missed a class that covered something important, or if you don't quite understand a term, concept, or assignment, there's still time to catch up, clarify, or ask for additional help. If the self-assessment comes too late — say, in the twelfth week of a fourteen-week semester — you don't have a chance to learn from the task and apply it to the remaining weeks of the course.

So at the halfway point, it's important to take stock of how you're doing in the class, what strategies are or aren't working for you, and what you need to concentrate on for the remaining weeks. For portfolio courses, your instructor may design a type of midterm exam that asks you to conduct an inventory of your working folder, to look both forward and back at your progress in the course, and to write some sort of self-assessment or reflective piece. A midterm portfolio provides good practice for the real thing and helps your instructor to determine a midterm grade for the course. Even without one of these requirements, it's an excellent idea to review your working folder and to spend thirty minutes or so writing a self-assessment, where you attempt to answer questions about your writing process, your strengths as a writer, and your preferences and habits.

TAKING STOCK #3: Assessing Yourself

Spend several minutes reviewing the contents of your working folder, including your plans, drafts, and postwrites. What patterns do you see in your own writing habits or approaches to assignments? Find one pattern in your working folder that shows something about you as a writer. At the halfway point of the course, write a short piece in response to your working folder and to the pattern you can see in your work so far. Discuss whether you think this pattern is encouraging or discouraging, and suggest how you want to address or change that pattern in the rest of the course. Meet with others in small groups to share your findings.

When asked to practice reflection and self-assessment, students often discover something about their habits or patterns that they had not noticed before, and sometimes they find areas where they need to work harder. Jen writes, for example, about her typical writing process: "I tend to write one draft, bring it to the workshop, then edit that one draft a little and hand it in as a final draft. I never spend a lot of time writing things over or revising my papers. This is a habit I still have from high school classes." Erin sees a lack of development: "I find that in my writing I have good ideas, but I don't develop them enough. I feel all my papers are good, but they need more." And Bridget admits that she isn't giving readers enough help: "I tend to leave things unclear. I assume because I know what I'm talking about that my readers should also." Each of these students identifies areas where her writing could use some work, and recognizing problem areas is a great place to start.

Journals, postwrites, or assessment assignments are just three possible ways of keeping watch over your learning. Practicing reflection throughout the course, through any method that works for you, will make this writing course more meaningful and will increase your chances of success when you pull the final portfolio together and present it to the evaluators.

—4—

Keeping Company, or Working with Others

A writer might work alone at a keyboard or alone in a library cubicle. She might need privacy and concentration to think, and she might invent original phrases or language. But that doesn't mean that writing is a solitary activity. Writers get their ideas from somewhere — from interaction with books, television, people — and they write for others; they write to be read. Writing projects are not completed in a vacuum; they grow from ideas that are planted or watered by others, through social interactions that may be educational or entertaining or both. In other words, the actual physical activities of writing may often take place in a lonely environment, but the mental activities of writing are heavily influenced by society and culture.

Being aware of writing as a social process will help you to imagine readers for your work and meet the needs of actual readers, like your instructor or classmates. In addition, as teamwork and collaboration on projects become more and more the norm in education and in business settings, working with others in a writing course will prepare you well for future collaborations or for the workplace.

Smaller classes that emphasize discussion, participation, and group work often become a community of students — with shared experiences, vocabularies, and concerns. A college writing class that relies on group work, for example, offers distinct privileges: You're aware of the history of the class, along with the inside jokes or stories; you know who is most helpful, or you feel comfortable asking for help; and you know you'll be missed if you're absent. Once you've become acquainted, read and discussed the same articles or chapters, worked through the same assignments, and generally shared the experience of working together, you and your classmates collectively have figured out a lot about each other and about what's expected in your course.

Any group that meets regularly and has a common goal or mission is bound to establish patterns of communication and different types of relationships. These shared experiences and familiarity, however, cut two ways: Communities offer the privileges of belonging but also insist on responsible membership. The idea that with privileges come responsibilities is one you've probably heard before.

To be a responsible member of a writing team, response group, or workshop classroom, you need to be prepared with your share of the work and ready to help others. You need to meet deadlines and give as much feedback as you get. But it is also important to be reflective or analytical about the group dynamics and behavior and to work toward making the group function more effectively and more supportively. In other words, you can practice responsible group membership if you apply the same type of reflection or analysis to your peer group as you would to your own learning processes — paying attention to how the group works and how it could work better.

TAKING STOCK #4: Assessing Peer Response

Analyze your most recent peer response session; that is, take it apart to see how it worked. Who participated, and in what ways did each member contribute? If you've worked with the same group more than once or twice, what rules have been established, consciously or not, about how your group is expected to work together? What patterns of communication are developing? What ritual activities does your group engage in?

If you were recently in a new group, what went well in the process of communicating, and what didn't? Did everyone participate equally? Write two or three paragraphs in response to these questions. Share your response with your group members, and then formulate a set of goals for improving your next peer review session.

The writing process is perhaps most social when it involves sharing your drafts with others and receiving their feedback. Courses designed around portfolios and the writing process tend to offer many opportunities for this kind of sharing and response, and you are expected both to seek and to give responses to your own writing and the writing of others in your class or response group. Even if class time does not allow for adequate responses or does not require postwrites, you can be a responsible group member by asking a classmate to exchange responses, perhaps via e-mail, or you can compose your own postwrites.

Whatever technique you use, make sure you don't skip this step of having specific questions for readers. Without having a plan for reader response, the response you get may be too vague or take too long because you're asking readers to do too much of the work. Do some of the work for them and you'll both gain more from the response process.

Becoming a good reader for fellow writers takes practice, and many students new to peer response groups struggle with what to say. The sentence openers in the following list assume that you are sitting with a small group of writers discussing your drafts, and that everyone has a copy of the paper. It will help the discussion if you can point to specific passages to illustrate your point. Try using some of these phrases or starters to break the ice in your next response group or to begin a comment that you find difficult to express:

- "I like the way you . . ."
- "What strikes me most about your essay is . . ."
- "Why did you decide to . . . ?"
- "This part made me [smile, wonder, feel sad]."
- "I wonder if you should move this part to here in order to . . ."
- "I get lost here."
- "I am surprised by this conclusion because I expected . . ."

Sharing your work and giving helpful feedback will get easier as the course progresses, and you'll learn the benefits of working with others to improve your writing.

—5—
Keeping Up,
or Getting Unstuck

The time you spend in class discussion, with your small response group, or on the Internet illustrates the side of writing that is most obviously social or community-oriented. Many of these social activities in your writing class will be in the invention or planning stages of the writing process, or in the revision stage when you make decisions about adding, deleting, or rearranging the text to better meet readers' needs. The time you spend in class brainstorming ideas, discussing readings, or sharing your writing contributes to the development of your sense of your readers and your responsibilities to them as a writer.

As you know, however, much of the work of a writing class takes place outside of class or without collaborators. When, for example, you leave the peer response group with a list of suggestions from your readers, you'll find that, despite all the suggestions, you alone must face the paper again. It's not unusual for the most experienced of writers to become stuck with a project, unable to make progress; however, you don't have the option of putting the text away until next week or month, waiting for inspiration to strike. You need to develop strategies that can help you make steady progress on an assignment or keep from getting hopelessly behind on a project. What follows are three situations that may or may not sound familiar to you as a writer, but the idea is to take your own stuck situations and find ways out of them.

GETTING STARTED

On a typical Wednesday during Lynn's first-year writing course, the class spends twenty minutes or so discussing a new writing assignment, which is to be a review of a book, movie, restaurant, performance, or exhibition targeted to an appropriate publication. Lynn's instructor emphasizes the importance of following certain criteria for the review, and the class generates a list of criteria for reviewing both a restaurant and a horror movie. Students ask questions about length and what newspapers or magazines would be acceptable to target, and then class time is up. Lynn is expected to report orally on her ideas for this review in class on Friday, and she'll need to have an initial draft for Monday's peer response group workshop. But Lynn is stuck. She prefers assignments that are more specific and give her few options; for example, she feels more confident with assignments that would require her to review a specific movie, assigned by the instructor, for a particular publication, also assigned by the instructor. She doesn't know where to begin in narrowing the topic.

What are Lynn's choices? She can hope that inspiration strikes in the next forty-eight hours, or she can stay a few minutes after class to ask the instructor for help. She can e-mail the instructor later that day, or she can call or stop by the instructor's office for a quick appointment. She can also go to the campus writing center, to see if a tutor has time to help her with the assignment.

Like Lynn, if you leave the class without a full understanding of the assignment, you're going to have to find the understanding somewhere, so take advantage of any available class time to ask questions or for examples or clarification. If you're confused in class but aren't sure what to ask, check to see that you have the instructor's e-mail address and office hours so that you can seek out answers to your questions as they materialize. If class time runs out and your question wasn't answered, stick around to ask the instructor your question, or see if a classmate has time to discuss the assignment further. Maybe the assignment seems clear in class but gets murkier when you first sit down to work on it. To sort through what's being asked, circle or underline the key words or phrases that signal exactly what's expected, especially the verbs. Look for such key words as *analyze, explain, illustrate, argue, support, show,* and *discuss.* For terms you don't understand, check the dictionary or textbook, and be sure to ask about them in the next class if you're still not sure. If the assignment includes an example, try to come up with another one that's parallel or similar.

Getting started with ideas and narrowing the writing task may take considerable time, but if that first step goes well, chances improve that the other steps will also go well. There might not always be enough class time for you to plan your paper or get ideas from others, so if you feel "all alone" in getting started, find ways to reach out for help.

PLANNING AND DRAFTING
MORE EFFICIENTLY

In the same first-year writing course as Lynn, Antonio is trying to develop new, better habits for writing essays. For many of his classes, Antonio has been able to write papers more or less the night before they were due. First he would write some notes and a quick outline in longhand; then he would draft the paper on his computer; then he would run the spelling checker and make a few sentence changes; finally, he would print it out to be turned in. But Antonio soon learns that his tried-and-true process isn't going to work for this writing course. For one thing, the topics or project assignments give him so much freedom that he cannot just "answer the question"; he has to find his own subject and narrow the focus. In addition, the instructor expects him to explore other invention strategies besides quick outlining and wants him to show evidence of invention in the working folder.

In his effort to break his habit of last-minute writing, Antonio tries some of these strategies that he finds in a textbook or hears in class discussion: He starts carrying a small notebook and pen in his backpack to be prepared to jot down ideas. Learning that ideas simmer in the back of writers' minds whenever they have a work-in-progress, Antonio uses napkins, receipts, and deposit slips to capture thoughts before they disappear again. Some writers, especially those who commute or spend a lot of time each day unable to record thoughts, will carry a small handheld tape recorder so they can talk through some ideas while driving, using time on the road to get "writing" done. After he's had a productive writing session — when the ideas kept coming and the words were flowing — Antonio takes a few minutes to try to figure out why he thinks it went so well. And when he's stuck, he feels free to stop for a while because he learns that many writers follow the practice of putting drafts away or turning to another project to give them some distance from a current one. Antonio also tries a technique for getting started again later; some writers will, for example, stop writing in the middle of a sentence so they will have a specific place to start the next day or for the next writing session.

Antonio also begins to depend on readers for his earliest drafts, sometimes called "discovery drafts" or "zero drafts," so that he can decide which direction to go in or which parts are the most interesting. He learns that readers are not just useful for fixing errors he didn't see but are also a good sounding board for his ideas.

SEEKING OUT OTHER READERS/
LEARNING ABOUT RESOURCES

Jasper begins his creative writing class concerned about whether his writing skills are good enough and worried that his work won't be up to par. Struggling alone with the first assignment, he wishes he had some way of knowing if he was on the right track. Then, during the second week of class, a tutor from the campus writing center comes in to give a brief presentation about the writing center's services. A number of students ask questions: Do they take walk-ins, or do you need a scheduled appointment? Does it cost money? Do they have an online tutoring service? How long are most tutoring sessions? What should I bring with me? What kind of help can I expect to receive?

Jasper learns from the tutor and his instructor that most colleges and universities have a campuswide writing center, where writers meet to talk about their work with other writers. These places are friendly and informal, with an atmosphere defined by the idea that "everyone is still learning to write." Writers at all levels and in all disciplines are welcome. It's not unusual, on a given day, to find a graduate student writing a thesis in microbiology, a budding poet working on verse for a creative writing course, a communications major needing assistance with a required course, or a graduating senior working on a résumé. Writing tutors or consultants are students, too, studying writing every day and still learning about it for different academic fields or to satisfy certain requirements. Most colleges and universities offer other tutoring or support services as well, often paid for by your tuition and fees. Even if you just want to use a good dictionary or have someone explain MLA documentation style, you can visit your campus writing center, and you can usually find someone there to talk with about writing or with whom you can share your writing.

Good readers can be found in many places other than your classroom. Even though your peer response group is the most obvious place to find readers, it's often a good idea to seek the advice of someone whose judgment you trust, especially if you prepare that person well with your postwrite questions. Friends, roommates, spouses, classmates in other courses, or tutors in your campus writing center may be good readers for you, too.

Finding Good Readers

Lynn, Antonio, and Jasper had different concerns or "stuck points," but every writer faces similar obstacles, especially when the writing is assigned and expected on a deadline. For many of the frustrating parts of your writing process, finding a good reader may be the solution to getting unstuck.

Who is a good reader? After sharing a draft with someone, ask yourself these questions:

- Do I *want* to work on this again? Can I imagine a starting place for revision?
- Do I know exactly what my reader suggested?
- Did the reader's reaction confirm my suspicions or fit with my instincts about what the paper needs?

If the answer to these questions is yes, then you've found yourself a good reader for your work, even if that person is not enrolled in your class.

TAKING STOCK #5: Working with Portfolios

Now that you've completed the first part of this text, what questions do you still have about keeping a portfolio? Do you understand or feel comfortable with the purpose of a working folder? As you begin the third or fourth week of your writing course, what are you feeling confident about and what concerns you? What role do you see the portfolio having in your effort to become a better writer? How can portfolio keeping teach you more about writing? List your questions, concerns, or comments in a journal or log and share them with your peer response group.

PART TWO

FROM PROCESS TO PRODUCT: PREPARING FOR ASSESSMENT

Like all processes, portfolio keeping results in a product — a portfolio suited to the purposes of your course and one of which you can be proud. Not all portfolio keeping includes an evaluation or assessment component, but for college writing classes, evaluation is undeniable; therefore the portfolio method tries to improve on that reality. Anticipating the final evaluation of your portfolio, then, we turn to analyzing and preparing for the assessment and the culmination of your portfolio keeping.

—6—

Understanding the Assessment Situation

One of the biggest challenges of writing well is to analyze the situation you're in as a writer and to decide, accordingly, how to present yourself and how to best reach and engage your reader. For the assessment of this portfolio, you are trying to convince an audience — a person or persons with more power than you have — to agree with you or give you satisfaction. Because you are faced with assessment or evaluation, the impression you make on your audience has palpable, measurable stakes. With every example you include or with every sentence you edit, and through a whole series of decisions you make along the way, you are affecting the outcome.

While this picture of the assessment may be intimidating, try to think of your portfolio as a situation that can be analyzed, broken down into parts, managed. Rhetoric gives us the tools for just that purpose.

Rhetoric, the study of effective communication, helps writers to analyze communicative situations that involve complex human reactions — situations like preparing a portfolio or assessing student writing. We wouldn't really need rhetoric or the study of communication if humans were always coldly rational and logical, if people didn't have memories, feelings, or associative thoughts, or if language were not often loaded, ambiguous, or dense. Rhetoric is for those topics about which there *can be* debate, disagreement, or differences. The skeletal system of a rat is not much of a rhetorical topic, but whether a politician is a rat *is* one.

The study of rhetoric teaches us the importance of situation and tries to break the concept of situation down into manageable parts. First, effective communication doesn't really begin until someone has identified a reason to communicate and feels compelled to act on it. When people feel the pull or need to say something, they take the first step toward engaging in a rhetorical act. The next step is to recognize some of the constraints involved — the obstacles, sensitive areas, or differences that may impede communication. In writing for college composition courses, the first stage, the need to communicate, is often handed to you; it is not one you discover on your own. However, once in a situation, whether chosen or assigned, your job is to try to identify the constraints and to shape your purpose, audience, and voice accordingly.

For portfolio assessment, your **purpose** is fairly clear: You need to convince your reader/evaluator that your portfolio represents your best work for this course, that you have succeeded in becoming a reflective learner, and that you have demonstrated writing abilities that fit with the highest standards of the course.

Your **audience** is, most obviously, the reader/evaluator of your portfolio — the person (or persons) who reads your work and makes a decision about a grade or credit. If the audience is your classroom instructor, you have an advantage. You've spent time with this person, have read the syllabi and assignments, have listened to lectures and explanations, and have participated in activities that this instructor designs and conducts. Therefore you have probably determined something about this person's values, preferences, or sense of humor. It is especially important, however, to judge not by stereotypes or careless assumptions but from concrete evidence whenever possible. A colleague of mine teaches in an electronic writing classroom where students study the implications of writing technologies on schools and workplaces. If one of her students were to assume, however, that she's a big fan of technology, that student would be making a serious misjudgment. This instructor uses technology to critique it and to help students become more critical and analytical about its uses and limitations. Based on evidence from the syllabi, assigned readings, in-class activities, and assignments, then, what information have you collected about your instructor that is based on evidence and reasonable conclusions?

Some portfolio assessments may involve an audience unknown to you — for example, an instructor for another writing class. If the audience is unknown to you, your decisions will be more difficult, but you can ask questions about your audience, and if you can make safe rather than careless assumptions, you can work with those. What would be safe assumptions for the audience for your portfolio assessment? Is it safe to assume that your reader(s) will be an educator — an instructor of writing, rhetoric, or communication? Can you assume that your reader is a member of the larger academic community at your college or university? What you cannot assume, of course, is personal information about your reader — for example, how long your evaluator has been a teacher — but you can imagine a reader who shares certain values, has a certain level of education, or is part of the writing or composition community at your school.

Once you have envisioned your audience, you can choose how best to approach that audience through your **voice**, or your self-presentation. What image of yourself (writer, student, thinker, learner) do you want to convey? What image would be most appropriate for *this* portfolio assessment? Self-presentation is somewhat easier when we are giving speeches: We recognize fairly easily that mannerisms and appearance — for instance, choice of clothing, hairstyle, and accessories — are important. Presenters or speakers make careful choices about their appearance depending on the audience and the formality of the gathering. But how does a writer present herself in prose without the advantage of visual cues?

The answer is that you have language, which is far more expansive than your physical appearance. How can your language reflect your understanding of your audience, of the situation, of the course material? You might try to demonstrate to your reader that you have successfully adopted the vocabulary of writing and rhetoric courses — that you can comfortably use the language of writing. In the courses I teach, for example, we talk all semester about readers and audiences, context and situation, focus, invention, genres, and revision — and I expect that students would be able to use these terms appropriately, along with others, in any conversation about writing. Similarly, I hope that students have begun to realize that a strong vocabulary and precise word choices are valued by many readers, not just their professors.

To present yourself as a careful writer, you need to find an appropriate level of formality in your language and become comfortable with it. Are you typically — in educational settings — a formal, private, reserved, or polite person? If so, your language might reflect that. If you are an easygoing, casual, relaxed, or calm person, your language can reflect that, too. Your choices about tone and level of formality will show up not only in your word choices but also in your use or avoidance of the first-person point of view.

TAKING STOCK #6: Looking at Language

With your peer response group, compare the following two passages of student writing for tone and language choices. How do the passages differ, and how can you account for the differences? What image of the writer do you get with each passage?

1. No, I am not obsessed with *Ally McBeal*, but I do believe that unisex bathrooms hold much promise for our society. Why not, for example, make the bathrooms of college residence halls unisex? A shorter trip to the bathroom would be appreciated for many reasons. First, I wouldn't get knocked over almost daily by a male who has waited just a little too long and now has an emergency that cannot wait. Another benefit is that unisex bathrooms would also reduce the embarrassment felt by the student who must walk through long hallways in her fluffy Winnie-the-Pooh bathrobe (her mother's choice) to get to the shower.

2. Some recent improvements to the city's image include Waterplace Park, a four-acre park surrounding a tidal basin. The park is edged by beautifully landscaped brick walks and a series of Venetian-style footbridges. Waterfire Providence, a dazzling display of fire and light that illuminates the water's surface, is held throughout the summer and fall. This new attraction aims to bring life and vitality to the capital city.

One way to think about choices of language, tone, and self-presentation is to ask yourself how much distance you want to put between yourself and your prose. Do you want to be close to your words or apart from them? How much do you want to own your words or stand behind them? Readers as experienced as your instructor will be able to tell if your language sounds hollow or forced, so try as much as possible to "be yourself." That's usually good advice for writing well and for other situations.

Most students understand the art of appearing studious or serious, eager or engaged, but make sure your language conveys sincerity because your reader will certainly detect overblown claims or pretension. Along these lines, watch your dependence on "thesaurus" words; they might not be used in a way that sounds natural. Unless you also consult a dictionary to double-check the words you choose, you could easily misuse a word.

No matter how carefully you attempt to craft your image — attending to tone and vocabulary and trying to match your language to both your personality and the context — a rhetorical situation can be more complicated than you might expect. No matter how well-prepared a writer might be, or think she is, some elements of the context are simply unknowable, or they change and shift. Your task is not to try to hold the situation still but to learn to recognize and then negotiate the changes it undergoes.

Understanding how rhetorical situations evolve and change, and how complex they are, will help you know how and when to intervene. Unfortunately, it is impossible to "know" everything about the situation surrounding the assessment of your portfolio. You cannot know if your reader got enough sleep the night before, or if he once had a very similar experience to one that you narrate, or if she knows more than you do about your research topic. The idea is not to guess your readers' backgrounds, beliefs, politics, or personal lives. Instead, you need to learn to make appropriate judgments about your readers as educated, intelligent, aware people who value reading, writing, and thinking — and what their reactions and questions might be as they read your work.

TAKING STOCK #7: Determining Your Program's Values

Knowing something about the values of the writing program at your college or university will help you to prepare a portfolio targeted specifically to its readers. If your college writing program has a brochure, pamphlet, or Web page that states the policies, expectations, and aims of the writing program, study that publication very carefully to determine what your writing program values about writing. Your portfolio will be evaluated based on the values of the writing program at your college or university. For example, a writing program that states an emphasis on classical forms of argument will read portfolios differently from a writing program that emphasizes personal writing and self-disclosure.

With your peer response group, determine what qualities of good writing your writing program values or is most likely to reward. Rank the qualities in order of importance, include a brief rationale for each, and then share your lists with another group or the entire class.

ASSESSMENT FROM AN
INSTRUCTOR'S PERSPECTIVE

Most writing instructors know, from their experiences as writers if not as teachers, how complex portfolio assessments are. When I enter the keywords "writing" *and* "assessment," for example, in a quick check of the ERIC database (for education), I get 6,836 entries. Testing specialists, composition researchers, and instructors at all levels of the curriculum find writing assessment to be one of the most challenging areas of our profession. Most writers, however, value assessment of their work — in the form of feedback, response, readers' reports, or criticism — if it is offered in the right spirit and if it helps them to improve a piece or to recognize patterns in their writing of which they had been unaware.

As a writer, I certainly find assessment invaluable — I couldn't write without readers who respond to my writing through a supportive but evaluative lens. I depend on readers to tell me where they find strong or memorable parts, where they get confused, and where they want more examples. As a member of my profession, I assess or evaluate the writing of my colleagues when journal editors ask me to review manuscripts. And as a teacher, I value and often enjoy assessing the writing of my students — helping them to sharpen the focus, solve an organizational problem, or see the most vivid passage. In none of these situations do I find grades helpful for assessment. When I submit my own writing for review, no one puts a grade on it, and when I review the essays of my colleagues, I don't use grades to express my thoughts about the text. When I respond to student drafts, I don't use grades either, but at some point in college classes, grades become inevitable. While grades are very "unnatural" to writers' processes, they are a very real part of some writing situations — like earning college credit. Grades are a necessary evil, and portfolios must be graded, too, when the time comes. For most writers, however, other forms of assessment are a natural and built-in feature of the writing process.

I make this distinction between assessment and grading because many students associate writing classes with being graded on every paper. After collecting a number of red-inked papers, students begin to believe that instructors just love grading their written work, that they relish circling or correcting errors, and that their sole mission is to show students where they are wrong. This may be true in rare cases, but most of the writing instructors I know don't fit this stereotype; in fact, they often struggle with grading and assessment because it's such a challenging and complex part of writing classes.

In the following section, I offer several typical myths about grading or assessment that you can check against your beliefs and experiences. How many of these statements have you believed? What are your instructor's views about these myths?

Myths about Writing Assessment

Myth No. 1.   Instructors love giving grades on written work; they find it easy to decide what the letter grade should be on any particular essay, story, or exam.

Actually, many instructors hate giving grades for writing assignments and often find it difficult to decide whether an essay should receive, say, a B- or a C+. Teaching students to write better is not like teaching them human anatomy, where all the body parts have a name and where test answers are either right or wrong. Writing has many shades of gray, and there are many right ways to succeed with a writing task. Every reader experiences a written text differently; even the same reader, on a different day, may have a response to something she didn't notice before. It's very difficult, in fact, to get instructors to agree on a single score for a paper; that's why a divergence of one point or one score is acceptable in large-scale assessments conducted by the Educational Testing Service (ETS).

Myth No. 2.   Instructors value only error-free prose. When they read, they look mostly at commas and spelling.

Readers, no matter who they are, are first interested in the ideas and look to be pulled in by the language and the train of thought. This is what instructors want, too: to be engaged in the ideas, the voice, the anecdotes, the examples, the pace. Instructors are readers, first and foremost. They love to read and want to read something good. If the writing is strong in other ways, readers probably won't notice lapses or problems. If the writing is predictable, undeveloped, or unpersuasive, however, then reading becomes stalled by grammatical, spelling, or punctuation errors. An intelligent, lively text can afford a few errors before it irritates instructors, but errors show up more if the text is unfocused or poorly organized.

Myth No. 3.   Instructors spend most of their free time correcting student papers.

It's useful to remember, as you analyze your portfolio assessment, that instructors reading your work are people, too, with a wide variety of interests and a lot of responsibilities. Besides leading full personal lives, college or university instructors also teach other courses, conduct research or write for publication, serve on department committees or national boards, and do other professional work. When your instructor sits down to read and evaluate a stack of portfolios at the end of a term, many other tasks are waiting. This doesn't mean that you and your portfolio aren't important but that you need to make an impression within a very small window of opportunity.

Myth No. 4. A letter grade is the only way or the best way to assess student performance in writing.

In your experience with school writing, you might have received letter grades more than any other kind of response, but there are other ways to assess writing. Most common are comments written in the margins or at the end of the piece. Other means of assessment include having a conversation about the writing, or what some instructors call a conference, that can take place in the classroom, hallway, or office. Instructors may tape-record their responses on a cassette that students can listen to at their leisure, or they may type comments on a separate sheet, without marking the text at all. For working writers, conversations about a written text also take place online, over the phone, or via e-mail, fax or voicemail. Whatever the method, effective response needs to be a conversation or dialogue, not a one-way street. The important thing is that ideas about a work-in-progress are exchanged and advice is shared and either accepted, rejected, or adjusted. Letter grades really don't accomplish this for a work-in-progress, although they may be appropriate for finished work.

Myth No. 5. Instructors are autonomous, independent, and can do whatever they want.

Instructors are not autonomous, even if they pretend to be. In obvious and subtle ways, their efforts are shaped or controlled by a number of institutional codes, rules, or guidelines. Instructors are not free to inflict any kind of torture upon you that they dream up, and they have to satisfy certain requirements, cover specified material, or undergo annual reviews. If they were autonomous, most would not give letter grades, knowing that the instructional value of grades is so questionable, but 95 percent of colleges and universities require that instructors give a single letter grade at the end of a term. That alone means that the instructor's assessment procedures are limited.

Myth No. 6. The evaluation of writing is purely subjective, and everyone is entitled to his or her opinion.

Because writing is such a complex act and language can elicit very different responses from people, it would be easy to think that evaluators are only being subjective when they decide that an essay is excellent, average, or poorly written. Readers do not develop their criteria for good writing in a private, personal way, however. Opinions come from somewhere: from one's experiences, from mentors, from the media. In a college or academic setting, most judgments are determined by the use of evidence or support; therefore writing is not judged from personal opinion but from a shared understanding of the characteristics of strong, effective prose. Teachers and evaluators of writing thus have developed a sense of good writing from years of reading (in their field and in the mainstream press), from listening to and working with colleagues, and from writing their own texts. While the criteria for good writing vary across fields and in different situations, such criteria are shaped over many years, through negotiations and social contracts that are usually subtle, implicit, or difficult to measure. Readers from *any* background rely on judgments that are neither purely objective nor purely subjective, but a little of both.

There are probably more than these six myths about instructors and assessment, but keep them in mind as you prepare your portfolio. They address a tough contradiction that teachers struggle with: how to encourage their students and help them to have a positive attitude about writing while also correcting and critiquing their work. It's a tricky line to walk, but what seems to help for me is a distinction between **reading** and **grading,** or between response and evaluation.

When I first sit down with student papers, *I am a reader.* Where does the text engage me, lose me, entertain me, bore me, or satisfy me? As a reader/respondent, my main focus is to give students the feedback and advice of an experienced reader, one who's done more reading and writing than they have. This kind of reading response requires **evaluation** — what works in the text so far and what doesn't. Not all forms of evaluation, however, include response. I could, for example, slap a big red C on the paper and be done with it. The letter grade would serve as evaluation but not as response, and most writing instructors agree that oral or written commentary is more instructive than a letter grade. Distinguishing between response and evaluation is tricky because some theorists claim that every encounter with a text or artwork is evaluative — that we are constantly evaluating something as we read it, listen to it, or look at it. Still, I think that acknowledging the differences between these two might help you to assess the stakes involved in different situations: *The situation will be different depending on the agenda of your reader.* Is your reader going to respond or evaluate or both?

For your own portfolio assessment — the reading and grading of your final portfolio — your reader is probably just going to evaluate and won't take the time to respond; that is, your portfolio will receive a grade and perhaps some brief marginal notations but not extensive commentary. This is largely due to time constraints, but it is also a result of emphasizing the importance of a product after the process has been completed. In other words, response should take place for a draft or a work-in-progress, but for a finished piece, it's appropriate to evaluate without necessarily responding.

Understanding the elements of assessment should help you to make enlightened, reasonable choices based on what you know and on what can be safely assumed. Rhetoric can inform those choices by giving communicators a set of tools with which to analyze the context or situation and to respond appropriately, reasonably, or judiciously. You will demonstrate your rhetorical understanding with each set of decisions you make about your portfolio, beginning with your choice of which pieces of writing should comprise your portfolio.

—7—

Choosing the Entries

Even if your instructor has assigned the number of entries you are required to submit, you still must choose which pieces to enter — and how much revision each one needs. Even in writing classes with very structured portfolios, you'll need to make a number of choices: Which essays and what types of changes?

Early in the course and in the first part of this guide, you were asked about your goals for the course and for your portfolio. This is the ideal time to review those goals and to make thoughtful choices about your portfolio that address or reflect some of those goals. The list of "Do you want to show" questions that begins on page 10 may be more meaningful now than it was during the first week of the course, and you may want to consult that list again to begin choosing your entries.

Let's review some of the questions that you may have been asking during the second week of the course but that now require real answers. Can you choose to include brief response papers, position papers, reaction papers, or one-minute papers? Can you include journal entries or impromptu or timed writings done in class? Does everything included need to be revised, edited, or both? The more you are eligible to include, of course, the harder or more time-consuming the choices will be, so find out as soon as possible the range of entries and what can be included.

SITTING DOWN WITH THE WORKING FOLDER

Once you're clear about what's eligible for inclusion or you have a goal in mind for the contents and appearance of your portfolio, sit down with your working folder in a place where you have plenty of room for spreading out the folder's contents and sorting papers. If you are using an electronic folder, open as many files as possible and try to arrange them so that they are all partially visible onscreen or can be easily minimized and restored. Here's where keeping an organized working folder pays off. As you pull labeled pieces out of your working folder, remind yourself what each piece is about (if you haven't kept up with the labeling and sorting, now is definitely the time to do it). In any case, familiarize yourself with what's there and do some initial sorting. Perhaps you'll want to arrange things chronologically, from the first piece you wrote for the class to the one written most recently.

TAKING STOCK #8: Reviewing Your Working Folder

As you begin reviewing your working folder, record your first impressions of your entire semester's work. Take some notes, at this point, toward the reflective essay or introduction. This is a good opportunity to jot down some of your observations or impressions: What surprises you? What patterns do you see? What would you want your instructor to know about all the work you've done that won't show up in the portfolio?

Use this session with your working folder to achieve two goals: to choose most or all of the portfolio pieces you want to pursue, and to make some initial notes about the reflective essay or introduction that you'll need to start writing soon.

To begin choosing the entries, consider your choices in light of the entire course and what has been emphasized about good writing. Also keep in mind the portfolio principle of variety. How much variety you can demonstrate will depend largely on the class and on your instructor, but review the handouts, assignment sheets, or other course materials for what qualities of writing the class has emphasized, and choose those papers that best illustrate those qualities. Reread or skim enough of your papers to remember what each was about. Reread quickly the instructor's comments or peer review forms, too, to try to remember as much of the context of your original draft as possible.

Once you have reread all of your essays or projects, you might want to begin a process of exclusion. Some students find it easier to identify the pieces they *don't* want to include than to pick those they do. You might start by setting aside the essays, projects, or pieces that you cannot imagine working on again. These are the ones for which you have very little enthusiasm, for whatever reasons. Maybe you didn't make good choices to begin with, or you lost interest somewhere along the way. Perhaps it's a project that always frustrated you and never did quite come together, or maybe the piece was timely two months ago but now seems dated or old news. Maybe you've become bored with the topic or think that you still have a lot to learn about the issue before you can write convincingly. In any case, how you feel about a paper is extremely important, and only you can determine that.

If you begin with the definite "no" papers, turn next to the easiest or clearest "yes" candidates. Which papers please you, make you feel satisfied, or are still interesting? Which ones do you catch yourself rereading from start to finish?

Notice that these suggested criteria for choosing the entries do not include "Which one did my teacher like best?" While such criteria may illustrate your audience awareness, the papers you like best are better choices because your instructor isn't the one who is going to be taking the paper through the revision, editing, and polishing stages. Because you have to live with this paper for the next two or three weeks, make sure it's one that elicits genuine affection or enthusiasm.

As you sort and review, definite "yes" and "no" papers will be the easiest to identify, of course, but the "maybe" pile might be the biggest. How do you decide among the possible entries in the "maybe" pile? Perhaps most important, you'll need to envision what each "maybe" entry will look like in its final version. A "maybe" paper doesn't have to be in excellent shape right now because there's still time to revise, edit, and polish — and that could be exactly what's expected. Your instructor has intentionally designed this course to give you time near the end of the term to revisit the writing process with each of your essays that show the most potential, and to finally finish the paper. Try sorting through the "maybe" pile with these options in mind:

- Choose a paper that shows promise or potential but one that still needs quite a bit of work; that way you can demonstrate your ability to finish a promising piece.
- Choose one that offers an interesting contrast to one or two of your other entries, or one that gives variety to the portfolio.
- Choose one that ties together two or three other entries, that provides a thread or common theme to your portfolio.

In general, use your own instincts and reactions to pieces to judge whether they should be submitted. If you can't get excited about a piece, how will you make your reader like it? If you're bored with it, your boredom will show. Readers will sense how you feel about these entries, so choose those that really get your writing juices flowing. In addition, choose entries about which you have something to say. If you can readily think of points you want to make about the project — about the writing process and how the essay evolved, or about why you wrote the essay, or what you think its strengths are — then it may be an excellent choice for inclusion. After all, you need to revise each entry but also be able to discuss why you chose it and what it demonstrates about your writing ability or your writing interests.

WHO CAN HELP YOU CHOOSE?

The people who know your work best include the instructor, of course, but also (and perhaps even more so) the peers or classmates with whom you've collaborated in this course. Without giving them any hints or showing them your writing folder, ask your most frequent group members which of your pieces they remember best. Their answers will tell you a lot about which of your essays had an impact or remain vivid.

You can ask the same question of your instructor: "Without looking at my writing folder, what did I write that you really remember?" Your instructor might be willing to answer that question, but many instructors will want you to make your portfolio choices independently, without much intervention from them. When my students ask me which pieces they should include, I might ask them questions like the ones just posed ("Which ones do you still have energy for revising?"), but I won't advise them about which pieces to include. It's now time for students to apply all they have learned about the rhetorical situation. After spending several weeks in a writing class — usually not a large group — and receiving numerous responses to your writing, you should recognize many of the values, preferences, and opinions of your teacher and classmates. This decision-making process is crucial to the learning experience of a writing course, and making the choices about portfolio entries is a rhetorical act, so most portfolio teachers will want to see that you can sort through the advantages and disadvantages of each choice on your own.

If all of your sorting and rereading still leaves you uncertain, talk to your instructor about other options. Maybe you want to write one of the projects or assignments again, but it would mean drafting a completely new paper. Your instructor might approve of that, but be sure to check first. Some instructors might not want any surprises in the portfolio, or they might need evidence that you have taken the paper through all stages of the writing process.

As you make your choices and prepare to revise and edit each piece, consider which one might work best first or last, and how the placement of each entry affects the whole. Because we know that first impressions are very important and sometimes lasting, it makes sense that the first few pages will be crucial in establishing your credibility as a strong, careful writer. Some research has, in fact, found that portfolio readers in large-scale assessments make their judgments very early in the process of reading the portfolio and that entries in the middle or at the end do not much alter the reader's estimation. The finding of this study, conducted at the University of Michigan, emphasizes the importance of a well-crafted introduction and suggests that your best entry should follow the introduction. But this study was conducted for "large-scale assessments," meaning that hundreds of portfolios were being evaluated in one session. If your situation differs, so might the outcome. You need to decide, of course, on the best order, and you may want to address the reasons for the order in the introductory piece. Whatever your decisions, your job in the introduction is to give some of the reasons behind them.

—8—
Preparing to Write the Introduction or Reflective Essay

Now that you've chosen the entries for your portfolio, what can you share with readers about your choices? What were key moments in the development of your selections? What do these entries illustrate about you as a writer? These are the types of questions you'll need to explore in composing the reflective component to your portfolio — whether it serves as an introductory letter or essay, prefaces each piece, or comes at the end. You've been practicing reflection since the first week of class, and now it's time to show what you've learned.

First, clarify with your instructor if you are expected to write an opening piece, whatever your instructor has chosen to call it. (Possible names include *cover letter, introduction, preface, reflective essay*.) If you are not being asked to preface the portfolio with a cover letter or reflective introduction, are you expected to describe your entries or introduce your choices in some way? Should *each* entry have a preface, in which you explain the changes you made or the process you followed in writing that piece? If your instructor has not assigned a cover letter or reflective essay, it could be that you've been asked to keep a writing folder and not a portfolio. But it could also be that some account of your choices or descriptions of your process are expected to appear throughout the portfolio — perhaps at the end or in brief introductions to each entry. The reflective essay does not have to be the first entry in the portfolio, but it often is, owing to its role in establishing a relationship with your reader/evaluator. Check with your instructor if its placement is not specified.

Whether a letter or an essay, this reflective piece could well be the most important text you will write all semester because it will show your ability to be a reflective learner and to analyze the rhetorical situation effectively. The introduction both introduces readers to your collection of writing and portrays you as a student writer. It explains your choices in compiling the portfolio and demonstrates reflection on your learning. For many portfolio-based courses, this document is a type of final exam: the ultimate test of what you've learned about qualities of good writing, about anticipating readers' needs, and about the importance of details — in this case, the details of a careful self-presentation.

TAKING STOCK #9: Revisiting Your Expectations

Go back to Taking Stock #1 (on page 7), on practicing reflection. Reread what you wrote about your predictions and expectations for this course and about the areas in which you thought your strengths would help you. Were you right? What from this exercise could you use in writing your cover letter or reflective piece?

If you have maintained a working folder and have managed to save, label, and file all of your paperwork for this class, now comes the payoff. Find all of the notes, postwrites, or log entries in which you've recorded something about your writing process, your struggles or triumphs, or the adjustments you've made in your writing or learning processes.

You have many options in writing an effective introduction — there is no magic formula or model text — but you will need to demonstrate reflective learning or self-assessment. In other words, show that you can evaluate the strengths of your work, that you understand what you do well and what you still need to work on. Instructors are not looking for perfection; they are looking for writers who are insightful, conscientious, and engaged in learning.

In the reflective introduction, you might try some of the following (but you can't choose all of these options):

- Discuss your best entry and why it is your best.
- Detail the revisions you've made and the improvements and changes that you want readers to notice.
- Discuss each piece of writing included, touching on the strengths of each.
- Outline the process that one or more of your entries went through.
- Demonstrate what this portfolio illustrates about you as a writer, student, researcher, or critical thinker.
- Acknowledge your weaknesses but show how you've worked to overcome them.
- Acknowledge the reader-respondents who have influenced your portfolio pieces and how.
- Reflect on what you've learned about writing, reading, or other topics of the course.
- Prepare your reader for a positive evaluation of your work.

One demonstration of reflective learning is being able to identify features or patterns of your writing process. Think of it this way: Readers of your portfolio have not been able to *see* your process. They haven't watched you write, haven't participated in your peer response groups, haven't seen all of your notes, drafts, and other evidence of your evolving ideas. They won't know what your friend suggested about the anecdote that opens your argument essay, and they won't know how hard you've worked on adding transitions between paragraphs. Readers will be aware only of what you share with them in the reflective piece.

Checklist for the Introduction or Reflective Essay

- Who will be reading this piece? Is the evaluator reading to suggest changes or reading to assess your work and make a decision about your effort and talent?
- What is the situation surrounding this reading?
- What will the reading's outcome be, and how much can you influence it?
- What qualities of writing will your reader value?

If your reader/evaluator is also your classroom instructor   Look back over the comments and responses on your returned papers and review the course syllabus and assignment sheets. What patterns do you see in your instructor's concerns or directions? Use what you've learned about your instructor's values as a reader to compose a convincing, well-developed reflective introduction or essay. It's doubtful that your instructor is looking to be flattered, and asking for an A is probably not the best strategy, but some humor, lively writing, or a charming anecdote might be very effective.

If your readers/evaluators are unknown   Ask your instructor to give you some information about your readers so that you can decide which logical, ethical, or emotional appeals might be most effective. In this scenario, you won't know your reader(s) personally (and they won't know you either). Still, it's safe to assume that your evaluators will be trained in portfolio assessment and will share many of your instructor's ideas about good writing. If your college writing program has a set of guidelines or policies and grading criteria, consult it for information as you begin composing.

If your classmates will also be reading the final portfolio   It makes sense that portfolios would be shared with the same people who have read and responded to your writing for the entire term, and you may be asked to make your classmates or peer response group your audience. In some classes, the portfolios may be shared with the group, but in others, peers may be asked to evaluate the portfolio. Because your instinct will probably be to write more informally for peers than for instructors, find out what levels of formality will be expected, or what uses of language will be most appropriate.

How long should the introduction or reflective essay be?   Check with your instructor for these types of details. Remember, however, that you need to develop your ideas or support your claims, as you do in any effective piece of writing. In this situation, you are trying to convince your reader that you have learned the course's subject matter and have also chosen wisely, revised judiciously, and edited carefully. If you are asked to write a *letter*, follow the format for a business letter (check your style and usage handbook) and include the date and inside address, as well as an appropriate salutation and closing. Above all, remember how important first impressions are, and don't neglect the importance of taking this piece through the same stages of the writing process that each of your entries has been through.

—9—
Revisiting the Writing Process: Revising, Editing, and Proofreading the Entries

While most stages of writing tend to overlap, revising, editing, and proofreading should be treated as discrete processes for improving the text. I find it helpful to emphasize to my students the differences among these three areas for improving a text. You have probably encountered revision, editing, and proofreading in other textbooks, or your instructor has reviewed them with you, and your working folder probably shows evidence of these stages. In any case, this section gives you strategies for sharpening your skills of rereading the text and finding places for improvement. One principle to remember is that any revision you do will create the need for more editing, and any editing you do will require proofreading. Each time you tinker with your paper, you need to attend to all three procedures.

REVISING

Revision literally means, *to see again*. The idea is to view the paper differently, from a different angle or through a different lens. When writers revise, they make global, wholesale, or fundamental changes in a text. Big changes, not sentence-level stuff. For example, Farah drafts a proposal to state lawmakers about raising the legal drinking age. When her peer response group agrees that lawmakers are not going to be convinced and that her points are too general, she revises the proposal by altering both the audience and the purpose: The revision is targeted to her university's president and proposes a change in the "dry campus" rules at her school. While her purpose remained "a proposal for change" and the topic stayed with drinking for college-age students, Farah's shift from lawmakers to her university's president allowed her to be far more specific and to cite examples from the campus community that her peer reviewers and the president would recognize and understand. Her proposal took on more specificity, greater immediacy, and a more local purpose, adding to its credibility and its potential success. As Farah discovered, revision is bigger and more involved than sentence-level changes: For her paper, revision meant writing an entirely new introduction to set a different tone, restating her purpose (or thesis) and adding far more examples. While she was able to save many of her sentences about responsible drinking, Farah's revising activities included frequent rereading, adding, deleting, and moving or rearranging parts.

Revision begins with the first reader, and that's you. Every time you read through a passage or paragraph, listening for places where you need to say more or say it differently, you are revising or considering ways to make the text more focused, coherent, or crisp. You may revise naturally and automatically as you compose because composing involves a series of pauses and rereadings. Each time you reread, you may find something to change, move, or clarify. Even though other readers — your peer reviewers, your instructor, your friends — will recommend certain changes, you should develop independent revising habits. Try to *read as a reader*, not as the writer or creator, and anticipate where readers are going to have questions or are going to want more explanation.

Many students consider revision one of the most challenging concepts of a college writing course. Many have not been asked to revise before, only to edit and proofread for errors. However, because revision is the foundation of portfolio writing courses — giving students time and opportunity to present their best possible work — understanding and practicing revision is a key to your success. There's a good chance that your instructor chose to use portfolios because they invite revision, almost insist on it, by providing a context for the revision — that is, end-of-the-course assessment.

TAKING STOCK #10: Assessing Revision

Review your working folder for evidence that you have practiced revision as it has just been defined or described — that is, making global or large-scale changes involving adding, deleting, or moving chunks of text. Where can you demonstrate your effort to revise? Write a short response to share with others about your understanding of revision, the efforts to revise that you found in your working folder, and your goals for revising your portfolio entries.

EDITING

Editing is another part of the writing process that you should be able to do independently even though you will also benefit from the fresh eyes of other readers who may catch lapses in syntax or usage that you don't see. Editing means working through the text in a systematic way, looking for places to tighten the prose and clarify the ideas with more precise word choices, varied sentence patterns, or different punctuation. It's important to remember that editing is about making choices, not necessarily about following rules. When writers edit, they make conscious choices in order to achieve a certain style or tone, for example, or to make certain features of the text consistent with the purpose or thesis. Editing is usually not as global as revision: Revision typically involves adding, deleting, or moving chunks of text, while editing makes the revised text smoother, more polished, or more cohesive. Editors often add key-word transitions or cut unnecessary repetition. A good handbook can help you with editing techniques, and some of the strategies listed in the following proofreading section can also help with editing. As with proofreading, the key to careful editing is to read differently from the way you read for content. Editing and proofreading both require that you change your normal habits of reading so that you can see the text differently. For example, when editing onscreen, you might change the background color and the color of the text. If you've been writing an essay using a gray background and black letters, change to a purple background with white letters. Such changes might give you a fresh perspective on the piece.

PROOFREADING

It's time for proofreading after you have revised and edited a text many times and your best judgment says that the text is finished, or you've simply reached a deadline for giving the piece to others. By the time proofreading is needed, however, you may have memorized the paragraphs and sentences. Therefore, the key to good proofreading skills is finding ways to see and hear the text differently or to break up the usual flow of reading, especially when you have reread the text from beginning to end dozens of times. While "seeing the text differently" may sound much like revision and editing, the target for what you're trying to see changes: For proofreading, you are trying to see errors and mistakes and flaws in formatting. That's it. The most straightforward of the three stages, proofreading asks you to find what is wrong with your essay or where you have violated social conventions for what a final copy should look like. When students talk about "fixing" their paper, they are usually referring to proofreading because the solutions don't involve making many choices. In contrast to editing, which is all about choices to improve the style, tone, order, or coherence, proofreading is about following conventions. You don't have to make many choices, but you *do* have to either know the rules or know where to find them.

So, with proofreading, your job is to find errors and mistakes, and again, distinguishing between these two will help. Mistakes are easier to find and to fix because you recognize that something must be done as soon as you see them. Mistakes are purely accidental. You say "oops," and then you make the correction.

Errors are more challenging because you often don't recognize them as readily — you may sense that something is amiss, but you can't identify it. While mistakes are accidental, errors show a lack of understanding or a lack of information. You never did understand the rule for using the possessive apostrophe with a plural noun (such as, "the commuters' lounge"), for example, and so you've omitted the apostrophe entirely. Errors and mistakes can be tackled through the same techniques, but rooting out the errors will take more time and diligence and maybe a helpful proofreading partner.

Here are some techniques that may help when it's time to edit and proofread the final entries for your portfolio.

- **Use a hard copy of the document, essay, or project.** Writing does not look the same onscreen as it does on a page. After revising and editing onscreen, printing out a hard copy is another way of altering the appearance of a familiar text so that you can see things you might be missing. Mark up the hard copy with changes that you can later enter on the computer.

- **Read aloud.** Try reading the paper aloud as though you have an audience, as though several people are listening and you are performing your text. Try standing up, projecting, and enunciating. How will this help when there's a good chance that someone who sees you will think you're crazy? Reading aloud helps you to hear the words, not just see them. Reading aloud helps to clarify your punctuation decisions and sentence lengths. Because reading your paper aloud is just plain different from reading it silently, your perspective will change — and that's all that many writers need to enable them to make improvements.

- **Read backwards.** Read backwards? Not word by word, of course, but line by line. This is very unnatural, and that's precisely the point. Because you've probably read your paper dozens of times from beginning to end, you are so familiar with the ideas and the sentence order that you are only skimming the text. You have, in fact, probably memorized the paper so that you know what comes next — and this doesn't help you to find the errors and mistakes. Begin reading backwards from the last sentence of the paper. Read up the last page and up the next page, sentence by sentence. The last sentence you proofread will be the first sentence of the paper. Why does this method help? When we read, we process chunks of meaning, without pausing for or recording every word; our powers of prediction and the repetition of the language patterns make it easy to skim or comprehend long passages without necessarily remembering every key word or phrase. For proofreading, however, you need to be able to see every mark of punctuation, every word. Proofreading requires a different kind of reading, but this will become easier with practice. (And you'll discover why good proofreaders are hired by publishing companies.)

- **Cover up parts.** Covering up some parts of the page to concentrate on others is a similar strategy to reading backwards: It breaks up the normal reading pattern and forces you to zero in on particular passages or paragraphs. For this technique, you need two blank sheets of paper. Lay them lengthwise, one at the top of the page you are proofreading and the other two or three lines down. The blank pages should cover up most of the lines on that page, leaving only a few others showing. As you proofread, move the blank pages down to keep as much white space as possible and to isolate the lines you're reading. How does this help? The marks on a page that constitute writing often begin to blur and run together, especially when a reader is tired or intimately familiar with the text. This technique of covering up parts reduces the lines of type a reader can see and creates more white space, which highlights the lines that are visible. Again, this changes your normal view of the text and therefore changes the way you see it.

Finally, as you proofread, don't forget to check all of the text's formatting. Are your page numbers or running headers correct? Are the titles for your portfolio entries correctly formatted? If a table of contents for your portfolio is required, is it correct and easy to follow, and do the page numbers match up? Consult a good handbook for many of these manuscript guidelines, or ask your instructor.

From the first page to the last, your portfolio should meet high standards. It should be a set of documents ready for public presentation, a product in which you can take pride and show others. Taking pride in your work means concentrating on revising, editing, and proofreading in the last days before the portfolio is due. In addition, some students find creative ways to give their portfolio that final touch or distinctive feature; for example, they have the portfolio bound or add a colorful or illustrated cover. For this assessment situation, however, it's important to remember that a cheerful cover, photographs, or fancy binding will not make up for weak writing or careless editing. Check with your instructor about any creative touches you may want to add because some instructors may object to this sort of adornment. In general, you can make the best impression by following the instructions and guidelines you are given, by investing time and care in your portfolio entries, and by making the most of the help, advice, and instruction you have received throughout the course.

—10—
Keeping, Continued: Encountering Portfolios Again

Portfolios are likely to increase in popularity and influence because so many educators find them compatible with the critical thinking skills they are trying to teach. It's likely, therefore, that you will encounter portfolio assessment in another course, for admission into a program, for an internship, or in a workplace. Even if you are not asked for a *writing* portfolio again, you may be asked for other types of portfolios, and the same principles of choice, variety, and reflection will apply.

Portfolios showcase an individual's learning and are extremely adaptable for classroom use, but they have also been adopted in large assessment situations, in which hundreds of students have their writing evaluated via the portfolio method. Some colleges and universities are using portfolios for long-term assessment or to test students for competency (perhaps as an exit examination to the composition courses). For example, the New Mexico State University first-year writing program requires portfolios for students that include four samples of their writing: a researched essay, an impromptu essay, a revision, and a reflective essay. These portfolios are assessed by faculty who teach the first-year course, and the results are used to evaluate the writing program and its effectiveness. Kalamazoo College in Michigan requires a portfolio for graduation. The class of 2000 was the first to begin keeping an electronic portfolio for all four years of their college experience, sharing it with advisors once a quarter and using it for reflection and decision-making. Maintained entirely online (through Web sites), students get experience with both electronic communication and portfolio learning.

Other forms of portfolios are increasingly popular at all levels of education. Graduate students earning master of arts degrees in English or other areas often have the option of compiling a portfolio in lieu of writing a thesis or taking a reading-list examination, and teachers-in-training or newly hired instructors often keep a portfolio that traces their progress as teachers. When faculty members apply to different institutions or are reviewed for promotions or tenure, they often submit a portfolio of their accomplishments in the areas of research, teaching, and service, accompanied by a narrative or rationale for each of their contributions to the portfolio.

During her senior year, Amanda, one of my former students, was enrolled in an internship program sponsored by the university. In addition to working at a local television station, Amanda attended weekly meetings with a mentor that prepared her for transferring skills learned in college to the workplace. Portfolio keeping was an important part of this internship. By the end of the semester, Amanda had collected and polished a portfolio that contained a copy of her current résumé, evaluations by her supervisors, journal entries about her experiences at the television station, and a brochure written to attract other students to the internship program.

As institutional, educational, and professional uses for portfolios increase and change, you may decide to keep your own portfolio — for writing or for other skills or interests — to track your learning or to record different stages of your development. Perhaps the self-motivated portfolio is the best kind because you create for yourself the opportunity or reason for portfolio keeping, and you become the best judge of your reflective learning. Whatever the purpose of your portfolio, good luck with it and all of the hard work and learning it will represent.